Salmos
FROM
SOUTH
BETHLEHEM

An Advent Memoir

PAMELA SMITH

Order this book online at www.trafford.com
or email orders@trafford.com

Most Trafford titles are also available at major online book retailers.

Printed in the United States of America.

ISBN: 978-1-4669-5094-8 (sc)
ISBN: 978-1-4669-5096-2 (hc)
ISBN: 978-1-4669-5095-5 (e)

Library of Congress Control Number: 2012914010

Trafford rev. 07/31/2012

 www.trafford.com

North America & international
toll-free: 1 888 232 4444 (USA & Canada)
phone: 250 383 6864 ♦ fax: 812 355 4082

Acknowledgments

Salmo #2 and #8 both made an early appearance in the *New York Quarterly* in numbers 13 and 14 (1972-1973).

Salmo #9 was in the *Cimarron Review* in 1973.

Salmo #13 appeared in *Woman Song III* (NRVC, 1989).

I am grateful to the editors of the publications named above for their interest in the work.

Thanks to Trafford Publishing and the efforts of Chris Toring and Jose Rodriguez, the full sequence of twenty poems from which these came is now appearing. The current collection has been updated, with an introduction and afterword added.

Dedication

With gratitude for street smarts, vision, and compassion, this collection is dedicated to those who peopled it forty years ago in Pennsylvania, whether by person or by mail:

Awilda Castañon, wherever she may be;
Padre Juan Campbell;
Bill Gasparrini, who still sends Christmas cards;
Louie, Uncle, and Helen, who live in fond and bemused memory.

Today it is for these South Carolinians:

Dee Rodriguez;
Jose and Karol Prado;
Nellie Lombardo;
Mary Bedient;
the performers in the Good Friday passion play at St. Gregory;
the bike rider from Puerto Rico who was collecting soda cans one Sunday at Alljoy Landing;
and a host of others who have brought their faith and culture across one or more borders.

Contents

Introduction

Rosa Celestina Morales

Just as it was some forty years ago, the south side of Bethlehem, Pennsylvania, is divided from the center of the city by the Lehigh River and the expansive brick buildings, smelters, corrugated ramps, loading decks, and smokestacks erected by Bethlehem Steel. The narrow, huddling, railroad-tracked neighborhood is edged on its own south by Saucon Mountain and the campus of Lehigh University. No one would have imagined four decades back that part of the steel plant would one day become the site of a casino, nor would they have guessed how much the university would reimagine a tumble-down neighborhood into more space for classrooms, labs, frat houses, and art centers.

In the early 1970s, the town was marked by ethnic neighborhoods and churches—Irish, Slovak, Wendish, Puerto Rican—and dominated by newsstands, mom-and-pop grocery stores, bars and grills, a one-screen movie theater, and luncheonettes like Helen's, where the aging, arthritic owner purchased, cooked, waited tables on customers in an impeccably starched uniform, and took her smoke breaks indoors. The Pennsylvania Railroad ran commuter trains to Philadelphia several times a day.

I was part of the graduate teaching assistant population, renting a front room from a blind store owner named Louie and his 90-year-old uncle who was known only as "Uncle." We shared the kitchen, the bathroom, and the side porch. I lived on hot dogs and sauerkraut, munster cheese and pumpernickel bread, raw carrots, canned vegetables, raisins, apples, coffee, coffee, more coffee, and an occasional splurge for supper at Helen's or El Caribe. The Fontanez family lived across the street. The parish Mass I attended every week was, from beginning to end, en español. Little by little I began to see the neighborhood and its neon nights through Spanish eyes.

Rosa Celestina Morales, the persona of these poems, is genuine in the reverse sense of poet Marianne Moore's "imaginary gardens with real toads in them." She is an invented 17-year-old citizen of the very real barrio that was Morton Alley, Fourth Street, Santa Infancia, and the approach to the New Street Bridge in 1971-1972. She's a composite figure, influenced by a Puerto Rican New Yorker named Awilda who used to write me letters about her yen to become a nun, as well as by the bilingual high-schoolers I passed every day. Some of her passion is akin to that of literati Piri Thomas and, later, Sandra Cisneros. Rosa's voice was drawn from a crowd of characters whom I overheard on hungry walks and met in narratives brought home by the social work student across the street who haloed his curly black hair with a leather thong as he sported sneakers and tie-dye and committed himself, for the time at least, to voluntary poverty.

These poems are Rosa's desperations and dreams, shaped as by funhouse mirrors and splattered with the cinders and soot of back streets. Like the prayers of the Hebrews of old, they are the uncensored uprisings of a befuddled, resentful, exasperated, and ultimately hopeful heart. They depict the inevitable collision of life and liturgy, day to day angst and elevated devotion. These poems have also, with time, become a memoir prayed in twenty earth-bound, local-colored salmos, psalms. The last piece of this collection is Rosa's sequel, a likely story of what might have transpired, in brief, over the years and what might have beckoned in a new millennium.

 **Salmo 1**

Siempre Manzanas
(Always Apples)

Mama
a river seeps along our street
the sludge of gutters underneath the patches here and there
of ice slick

Louie our landlord who cannot see
thinks there are still apples bulging off a backyard tree
everywhere anywhere
los gatos creep

Cain and Abel Adam Eve
I hear stories at church and think
                    good food and bad bad seed
my brothers and sister sometimes wet the sheets

and always I am somehow worse when I hit where we live
upstairs in a punched-in house near no one's street
                litter cinders bottles brick chips
                cigarillos fruit pits dogshit

1

my tight throat chokes where shadows fall
and suddenly a swish of feet
                  a puff
                            the smell of hair and joven grease

Madre, santa,
los borinqueños mis hermanos
                  they hoot and howl at me
                  catcall

                  --mama ven conmigo—
                  --conmigo—
                  --conmigo—
pero no ronroneo
yo no ronroneo

but then
I scurry down the street
they catcall
                  --psst psst—
                  --ven aqui—
                  --o ven acá—
                  --here kitty kitty—
                  --miz—

ellos (they!)
los gatos machos
tom-tom-tom their boyhearts beat
those tomcats

lounging

licking

> --here sissy sissy—
>
> (kiss kiss kiss)

skulking like alleycats
mousing
smooching to themselves

and I scat down the street
scaredy-cat

> --miz—
>
> --miz—

past Maio's fruit stand

> --o las manzanas—
>
> his tightwad widow cries
>
> --pero ni naranjas ni mandarinas ni peras siquiera
>
> and yes we have no bananas
>
> the drought you know and then the freeze
>
> pero muchas manzanas siempre manzanas
>
> for you dirt cheap—

(and worms)

(such
truly
happy
juicy
worms)

so here it is late November
and all along the river bank

nothing but the swollen trunks and snaky limbs of trees
and the last limp yellow leaves

and an old mother
una vieja carcomida
inches along the sidewalk
muttering to herself

and biting her lips
                              --here pussy pussy—
as if the skin
is all she has to eat.

Nuestro Pan de Cada Día
(Our Daily Bread)

Emmanuel
         (hijo)
I have seen my father naked and drunk

thirty-eight and out of work
lost in the curls of his fat mustache
lounging by the curb he flirts
              --chick chick—
while in Carraquillo's kitchen mother cooks
morning afternoon and night

and I
I boil beans and rice

        hermanitos hermanita
        Orlando Luis y María
        home for lunch (con apetito)
        arroz y habichuelas
        arroz amarillo y habichuelas rosadas
        rice and beans

yellow pink
o arroz blanco y habichuelas blancas
(tipo puertoriqueño)
rice and beans
white white white
cocidas en agua y sal
boiled in water and salt
morning afternoon and night

Orlando Luis and María recite
the only prayer in Spanish they know
--Padre nuestro que estás en el cielo—
--Padre nuestro—
--Padre nuestro—

thirty-eight and out of work
lost in the curls of his fat mustache
our father tinkers with an old used car
warms his hands with his November breath
tells dirty jokes and winks at Gloria Vasquez
teaches Pablito down the street to curse

Goya beans and rice
bought at the rundown Puerto Rican Price-Rite
--Padre nuestro que estás en el cielo—

Papa tools his hot rod
buys a glass-pack muffler at Auto Boys
to make more noise
and sticks the roadrunner decal
--meep meep—

next to ¡Puerto Rico Mi Encantada!
on the dented bumper

Papa loves his glass-pack muffler and the roadrunner trademark
like a child with toys in a magic toybox

        Orlando Luis y María home to eat
        arroz y habichuelas y y y
        beans and rice and rice and beans

while our father the steelworker six months laid off
hands out beer four six-packs on the house
our father's hot rod full of deadbeat spicks
jiggling bottles of Corona cerveza one in each fist

        our papa
        and Pedro Felipe Enrico José
        jiggling beer bottles
        --ha—
        like maracas

while in Carraquillo's kitchen mother cooks
(con cucarachas)

and morning afternoon and night
I boil beans and rice
        Orlando Luis y María home to eat
        --Padre nuestro—
        --padre—
        this day
        --danós hoy nuestro pan de cada dia—

bread or rice and beans

thirty-eight and out of work
our papa flirting tinkering joking drinking
spends one two three four five six dollars' worth
of mother's checks on God knows what
but not a slice of meat

Emmanuel
(hijo)
I have seen my father naked and drunk
                    rice and beans yellow and pink
                    our mother at table stove and sink
I have laughed and laughed
laughed myself sick
laughed my stomach into its pit.

 **Salmo 3**

¿Y en la Tierra Paz?
(And on Earth, Peace?)

this morning this young woman
me –ay, ay–
humming gloria a Dios en el cielo
glory to God in the sky
walking to uptown
crossed rio Lehigh
then changed her tune and sang to herself
--noches de angustia–
like T 6 for 10¢ at Carraquillo's

and why

because a crowd of school age brats
playing hooky and goose stepping four abreast
goose stepping goose stepping three rows back
a dozen white junior high creeps
like hepped up storm troops or crazies loose from the hoosegow
marched into me on New Street's under construction bridge
marched into me purposely
nudged me to the bridge walk

poked /
kicked /
giggled /
stared at their feet /
chuckled
showing me their snide teeth /
nudged me to the side rail
(rickety rickety) /
half crushed my chest /
like jackasses who bray and balk
and pause gassing and angry where they please

and I

(whoa)
--ay de mí—
I stood stock still
my wind knocked out
until the dozen desperaditos
desperadodos
all pimpled stinking of sweat
foul-breathed and tight-pantsed
passed by the laughing hard hats
• rat a tat tat •

and I who never cry
turned back bewildered to downhill uphill Southside
mumbling y en la tierra paz
a los hombres que ama el Señor
(dead water below and frozen mud)
and on earth peace to men who love

10

I who never cry
sidled stunned into restaurant El Caribe
where chuletas asadas were the special of the day
--ay de mí—
and I who never cry slumped into a far back booth
by the pinball machines and juke
sighing tú que quitas el pecado del mundo
--you who take away sins—
I bummed a cigarette
a Kool
and slouched like a ragged floozy
tore from my coat the buttons that were loose
rubbed where I was scraped and bruised
my ribs my shins
smoked muttering a curse
and two
(sadly shaking his head at the cash box glanced Señor Carraquillo)
so I said café con leche without even por favor
and like an icehead penguin
I went into a brood

thinking God o God deliver me
from coldblood white trash enemies
from giddy stupid school kid brutes

in a haze of smoke I dreamed
their flour paste faces swollen and stiff
their skinny pink lips puffed and stitched
sweet Jesus perdónanos perdóname
but if cauliflower ears and broken teeth
if I would see (o God forgive)

11

those little jackbrats not spanked and slapped
not scolded and fined
but ganged up on
wasted
trashed
pulp-beaten
slashed and scarred from ear to ear
I might heehaw and jeer like a drunk muleteer.

 *Salmo 4*

Ten Piedad
(Have Mercy)

on my bed I flop
I talk to my own heart
   --Señor ten piedad—
   --Cristo ten piedad—
when I pass by
the childmen watch
as if I flounced in a skin-tight skirt hemmed up to my hips
as if I wore red lips
as if at night I lounged on the sill of my window
lolled above the sidewalk
drooped
folded my arms like estúpida Alma
as if I never pulled my shades
as if I lay watching tv
in a lacy negligee
and patted my pudgy tummy
while I slurped from a pull-tab can
another Rolling Rock beer
     ¡olé!
as if I rose and rose again to see from my second storey

who was looking across the way
as if I went to the window by the fire escape
to lean out to a boy who swaggers down the street
clicking his Cuban heels with cleats
to wave

> --joven
>
> ojo mi novio
>
> joven come up
>
> ten una cerveza
>
> much beer I got—

when I pass by

> ¡olé!

those tontos make of me mincemeat

once when I was seven
and new in the parish here in Belén
once when I was seven
I stopped by the church
and saw a woman at the altar rail
kneeling with her arms outstretched
as if she was being nailed to a cross
she knelt and prayed till her crucified arms
twitched
shook
collapsed to her sides
as if she almost gave up the ghost

> --Señor ten piedad—
>
> --Cristo ten piedad—

and ever since and again and again

I see her or someone or anyone
some woman in a dark mantilla
praying that way
and I
I shiver and jerk
for I can almost feel the spikes driven through her hands
I can almost see a roughneck soldier scowl and lift his mallet
almost see him lift · hit down · lift · hit down ·
I can almost feel the spikes drive through her hands
ever since and again and again

o God those sillygilly men
those dopes who loiter around Domenico's news stand
o God I ask
           las pesadillas

                paws
am I a halfwit with the heebie-jeebies
or a holy woman taking up her cross?

 **Salmo 5**

La Temporada Gravida
(The Pregnant Season)

I wake up ravenous and glad on the first day of December
mi mes favorito
la temporada gravida
(la madre de Cristo)
grinning how happy I am and hungry

diciembre
the trees
               elm black walnut oak
whose limbs don't need a stitch of clothes
whose topmost twigs don't smell morning coffee boiling on a gas
burner stove
diciembre
when jumping awake on such a day is breakfast itself
the alarm clock and morning frost

lightly lightly

out of bed I shimmy from pj's into underthings and slip
and dress like a bough of holly

red in my plaid and yellow and green
and think I should make up a song
like God rest ye merry cheerios
o come all ye flapjacks
deck the halls with plates of pan fries

I am so unreasonably hungry
sunnyside eggs in old fatback grease with lots of pepper and salt
o little town of
one cup of coffee two cups three
Bethlehem in Pennsy

diciembre
a morning like breakfast
a morning like a cedar chest or a mothballed closet
a morning frost

adviento

and my morning prayers all mixed up
when I think María was plump and Jesús still inside and bunched up
and the Israelites sick of waiting for Mesías
knocking themselves out to pay taxes while the Romans took
census
and José
pobrito José

I am a fizzbrain like this only at daybreak
en diciembre diciembre
because before I can decide whether to sew up a little hole
in my almost ancient pantyhose

and buckle my wet-look patent leather shoes
I am humming a high school Spanish song about burros
and thinking about Mexican jumping beans
and coffee coffee coffee
and how I wish I had a fiancé

because before I am downstairs the telephone rings
to tell my mama that Rosa's plastic curtains were open
and her shade halfway up
and she was just sitting at the window daydreaming
dressed only in her slip and her room all lit
in the very unholy halo of the lamp on her little night table

our fuddy-duddy old sourpuss aunt
la solterona
la solterona oficial de toda la familia
our skinny scarecrow aunt who lives unfortunately across the street
our worldwide expert gossip
our aunt who looks like a horse they forgot to feed
la boca grande with gumless teeth and hollow cheeks
our aunt who looks like a mummy
de quien la boca es una sepultura abierta
is calling as usual to fuss about her nice the nincompoop
(who has sometimes the strange habit of happiness)

and to chew the fat of the barrio news.

 **Salmo 6**

Confesión
(A Confiteor)

Rosa Rose o santa o
the thorn in my flesh
my body is in terror
my bones are vexed
(is it only growing pains as in an old wives' tale
or is it worse
the night visiting diablo)

         solo tú

I am afraid of how I ache

        allí allí

and how I tremble when I dream
and when I wake from such a dream
so weightless and too scared to scream
as if pebbles thrown against my window woke

            tú eres piedra

as if footsteps on the stairs
as if at the door a click
blood and circles round the moon

         the end time is it soon

so soon

blood and circles round the moon

the tear stain
(holy saint of Lima how long)
the blood drop

how I tremble when I wake
I am afraid of how I ache
Rosa Rose a mí
the thorn in my flesh

yo confieso
yo confieso ante Dios todopoderoso

when tossing off my sheets
I nightmare Pedro
I tiptoe double quick
I think of Pedro
his hard heart

I check the bolt
I check the lock
Pedro
rock
and I quake

que he pecado mucho de pensamiento

the moon is full

por eso ruego a Santa María siempre virgin

I am afraid of how I ache
I am afraid of how I wake
shaking kidnapper rapist molester thief
o Pedro of the dark and dead stop of my heart
I do not know

blood and the drop drop drop of the moon

how you can steal into my sleep.

Salmo 7

¿Una Caña Sacudida por el Viento?
(A Reed Shaken by the Wind?)

San Juan Bautista
la voz que grita en el desierto
I lose my head
pierdo la cabeza
porque
day after day and again today
I am mocked
        --hey mulatto—
        --you nigger or what—
I Puerto Rican am pure hodgepodge
white and black and brown and white
Spanish conquistador
African slave
Aztec or Maya
a trader from Georgia
(land of the free
home of the brave)
by whom my greatgrandma in 1898 was they say mislaid
        --hey mulata ready or not—
        --hey bastarda you cold you hot—

San Juan Bautista lift your voice
(for my thin skin)
San Juan you bag of bones
        (for me)
        (for sticks and stones)
make noise
        (for those who break)
shout locust tough and honey sweet
shout down
o drown them out

what please do they see
a white tarbaby
a chocolate drink
        --una caña sacudida por el viento—
        --un hombre vestido con lujo—

o desert dry and water crazy
just me
señorita half-breed simpery smiley
good looking and loca
too thick to think

o deep in my hurt can I help that I fear
what if the voice is a windbag
what if the prophet is punch drunk

San Juan Bautista la voz que grita

San Juan I hope
        (in a man in wild clothes)

(in a man eating bee-sweet grasshoppers and trees)
(in a man who is God-mad and strange born)

Patrón

I hope
        (in a man crying out –todos veran--)
that I that we may see
        (in the wilderness where we wait)
           (the blind)
           (the lame)
           (the heartbroken)
when the hills cave in and valleys climb the sky
when the poor overflow and the rich run dry
when the God of multicolor and God of many tongues
calls me woman not thing
when that God comes

but oh if that head on a dish is nada
the mask of the man in the moon
if that wonderful cry
           --elevense—
is the last gasp whisper
(o la volada)
of a helium balloon.

 **Salmo 8**

Poco Menor que los Ángeles
(A Little Less than the Angels)

what am I

        baby spit and sour milk vomit

that when I look at the moon and stars in the sky

I wish

        ave

to kill the animals

        Dios te salve María

I wish

to damn the land and man

        bendita tú eres

        entre todas las mujeres

yet at the same time chant

gloria gloria gloria

        madre

        mujer

to shelter

to bear

        bendito es el fruto de tu vientre

for I have outgrown my days

I have sighed past my years

dieciséis
diecisiete
diecio . . .
this waste

what am I
that when I hear the clatter of sleet on a sick December night
I think
--el angel del señor anunció a María—
--y concibío del Espíritu Santo—
the whines of stray cats scooting from spot to spot out back to hide
sound so much like babies' cries

holy Mary mother of God
the other day from Señora Luz María Padilla de Calderón
I heard of a man and wife
who put their infant in a buttered pan
set her on the kitchen stove and lit the gas
and sat down to listen to a baseball game
until the neighbors next door could no longer stand
the wailing they heard as the infant fried
that they called the police
--policias—
who drove up in a black maria
battered down the door
arrested the two poor whites
and took the tiny girl to have skin grafts on her backside
placed her in an orphanage by court order
where she was visited by a special doctor
who has tried for ten years
tried for ten years to reach her

begged her for ten years to touch someone
to bawl
to laugh

why Señora Padilla de Calderón
am I glad for sheep and cattle
all wild animals
birds and fish
all deep sea beasts
but sick to death of grown women and men
why Señora Padilla de Calderón
why Luz María
do I smell soft snow of baby powder
and taste a warm dewdrop of carnation milk
   the earth
    the heavens
and know that I could be some niño's mother
but wish I was a child again

Holy Mary or Mother Goose
what am I
    baby spit and sour milk vomit
that on a night cold as the snow queen's palace of ice
     in an old Walt Disney cartoon
I want hey-diddle-diddle wallpaper with a cow jumping over the
moon
I a seventeen-year-old girlwoman
   --he aquí la esclava del Señor—
   --hagase en mí según su palabra—

o what

that in the middle of a sleet storm
I imagine that the racket on the lids of trash cans
is the dosey-do of a cat and a fiddle
the clackety-clack of a little dog laugh
and a dish run away with a spoon.

Salmo 9

La Esperanza de los Afligidos
(The Hope of the Afflicted)

when I am a bowlegged old lady
toppling roly-poly down the street
with a bag of groceries
(still eating eggs and cheese instead of meat)

when I am a bowlegged old lady
wobbling side to side like a top
while I wait chilly and tired at the bus stop
(still having trouble warming my feet)

I wonder will I still light blessed beeswax candles
and burn them for a quarter
will I still pray to so many saints and martyrs

(Juan el Bautista
Esteban
Matías y Bernabé
Ignacio y Alejandro
Marcelino y Pedro
Felicidad y Perpetua

Agueda Lucía
Ínes Cecilia Anastasia
y todos los santos)

after housework and do-it-yourself
bowlegged
as if I had straddled a sawhorse

will I still give up chocolate for Advent

(Dios es nuestro alcázar en tiempo de peligro
confien en ti los que conocen tu nombre
Tú no abandonas a los que te buscan Señor)

after lovemaking and children and children
bowlegged
as if I had been a wheelbarrow

will I still genuflect and kneel before the altar
will I still sing psalms with my sisters and brothers

(no te olvides por siempre del pobre
la esperanza de los afligidos no quedará frustrada
levántate Señor que no triunfe el hombre)

when I am a bowlegged old lady
still shopping waiting and praying like a chatterbox
I wonder what o God it will be worse to be then

a woman
        a Catholic
                half black
                        or Puerto Rican.

 *Salmo 10*

Para que No Vuelva a Aterrorizar
(Just So He Doesn't Terrorize Me Anymore)

Pedro with the red hots
like he ate everything with too much tabasco sauce
Pedro with the red hots
ants in his pants
las hormigas rojas
I love and hate

he jimmies and jars the pinball machine
Pedro who snaps his fingers and slaps
when the numbers by the girl in the bikini light up
Pedro jumps and jiggles like a jitterbug
handshakes and heeltaps
like a man con el ataque
        o Virgen de Guadalupe
        Pedro de los dedos prestos
        Pedro's fast light fingers
        o keep off me

as usual he smells like cheap wine or whiskey
      --este vino

fruto de la vid del trajabo del hombre—
Pedro digging into a plate of habichuelas con verdes with a spoon
Pedro eating with his fingers pollo barbecue
harangues
(beans with snaps and chicken barbecue)
about dignidad y respeto
like a Puerto Rican papa
home from the sugar cane fields
to say grace and break bread with his wife and children
    --este pan
    fruto de la tierra y del trabajo del hombre—
Pedro with the red hots shouts politics for three minutes
then chachas off to the jukebox to fill the coin slot
por Orlando Contreras
y los discos
      --me haces pensar (M 2)—
      --de donde (M 3)—
Pedro cracks a sleazy joke
    (me haces pensar)
and bebops back to the pinball machine
    (de donde)
eyeing lustfully me
as if I should jump up in my open-toed clog-heeled shoes and stomp
like señorita la bailadora with a rose in my teeth

for Pedro el hombre con machismo
the lord of the dance
    (M 2 and M 3)
the way he raises his eyebrow and cocks his head at me
Pedro who could be a pickpocket
    a bookie

a pimp
Pedro who may be a junkie or a speed freak at least
his sweat
his whiskey and cigarette breath
the aroma of spice at el Caribe
his face
the taino
the Spaniard
the slave
Pedro who makes me sick

but fascinates.

# Salmo 11

A la Misa del Segundo Domingo de Adviento
(At the Mass for the Second Sunday of Advent)

if I am a bird
a little bird
they are bowmen
who string their bows
and set their arrows on the strings
and let them fly fly

       ·spick·spick·spick·spick·

even in the dark
they aim deadeye

several years ago one March
down a dusty hallway
of a tenement
on the outskirts of the city
a haggard Jewish lady
sang a strange Ladino song
--los bibilicos
ca
  a
  a

an
tan—
la señora judía
(an old yid spick hen)
la señora judía
singing a faraway weird song

> (desde sión la hermosa
> Dios vendrá a manifestarse)

the bowmen sport
yes sport with me

> ·spick·spick·spick·spick·spick·

and today
a la misa del segundo domingo de adviento
el himno

> --oh ven oh ven Emmanuel
> libra al cautivo israel—

an old Spanish jewess

> --que sufre desterrado aquí
> y espera al hijo de David—

came
came back

that March

> (I've heard of nightingales
> and gray nightjars)

an old Spanish Jewess
cooed me off to sleep

and on the lullaby
I learned to fly
over mountains
treetops
lowlands
to the Caribbean Sea
San Juan
my wing
my wild bird's eye.

Amigos
(Friends)

I am much upset

because today when Orlando who is ten
went to the door to answer the knock of his boyfriend
they gave one another a rowdy athletic hug
Orlando laughed and knocked off Ricardo's cap
they gave each other a rap on the back
a love tap

> mmm-hmm
> mi amigo
> mi
> he

and then he who is ten got his jacket and mittens
and went to play football in the street

with my girlfriends I shop
we go to games and at school sock hops
we gab on the telephone
giggle and girltalk around our mamas in code
but we are proper flower pots

we prettify and hide a lot
we are secret stuck-up touch-me-nots

and so I am
                    whoever listens in heaven
jealous of a boy who is ten
he has intimates
confidantes

today I feel like a pigskin
blown up with hot air and rah-rah

then kicked.

 **Salmo 13**

Mamacita
(Little Mama)

her sleeves rolled back
her sturdy housewife arms loving and rough
my mother
heaves the kitchen window up
and tosses out some stale bread crumbs
to winter birds who do not worry
in this land of milk and honey

> give give us this day
> our bread our manna Lord hosanna
> nuestro pan de cada día
> dános hoy
> dános hoy
> oh when will bread fall from the sky
> --mi paz os dejo
> mi paz os doy—

> > a little while
> > in just a little while

as little as prints in the snow of sparrows' feet
as little as the junco Mama watches
flitting from limb to limb of our bare crabapple tree
as little as her pinched winter smile when wrens
light in our narrow backyard to feed

as brief.

 *Salmo 14*

Toda Tu Familia Santa
(All Your Holy Family)

bickering
nosepicking
los niños   María   Orlando   Luis
dickering

              (con Señor Gomez al mercado)

over coffee

              instant or ground
              chicory or not

mi madre

cigar chewing
coin flipping
mi padre

toda la familia

              (acepta Señor en tu bondad
              esta ofrenda de tus siervos
              y de toda tu familia santa)

slouched over the sofa in front of tv
        (ordena en tu paz nuestros días)
or lolling on the popped-spring cushions and arms of a living room chair
        (líbranos de la condención eternal)
reading Bazooka Joe gum wrapper comics or the Double Bubble
fortunes during commercials
        (y cuéntanos entra tus elegidos)
Saturday afternoons
Bugs Bunny   Porky Pig   Woody Woodpecker   Looney Tunes
this whole family
hickory dickory dock

this whole family makes me sometimes think of drunk Hernandez
and how I found him one night
down where they were blockbusting apart
the shoemaker's
the barber's
and the candycigarettesodapopsomethingforeveryone shop
to clear the way for a parking lot
of drunk Hernandez
and how I found him collapsed in the display window
of the next store in the row to go
a store already halfway boarded up and barricaded
Hernandez dressed in nothing but greasy slacks
shirtsleeves
and worn-through shoes with no socks
lying like a baby bird in a smashed egg shell
after a tree shook in storm winds and the nest fell
Hernandez in a mess of shattered glass
Hernandez bloodless and hardly dressed one October night
when it was 50° or less

how I tried at least six times to wake him up
of drunk Hernandez
and how I picked my way tiptoe through the broken glass and
rusty nails
finally to touch his arm / shake him / insist
  --Hernandez Hernandez mira
  respóndeme
  mira Señor—
like a birdmama come back to a topsy turvy tree frantically
shrieking
  --mi pueblo—
  --mi pueblo—
till he mumbled he was sick and I should phone the cops
  (que devoran a mi pueblo
  como si comiesen pan)
and I did so
of drunk Hernandez
and how after I got out of the pay phone booth I wanted to upchuck
and headed with Hernandez a little down the street

so when Felipe at the grill in the Blue Heaven hotdog shop
said that in the hoosegow Hernandez would get a hot meal and maybe
a shower and warm blankets on his cot
and meanwhile he would check Hernandez for cuts and bruises
and sit him on a stool with some coffee and watch

before the cruiser came I got lost

and sometimes this whole stupid family in this mess of a love nest
a rat's nest
(juzgado the jailhouse)

reminds me of Hernandez smashed in the window case

at the front door María in her underpants doing a hula
while Orlando bops her on the noggin with a left out mop
on the floor with a hole in the toe Luis's smelly socks
upstairs my mother swallowing aspirin
          crushing her head into a pillow
                    and snoring this afternoon by one o'clock
my father somewhere up or down the block
and on the living room table top from just before Mama got home
          cigar butts
          beer bottles
          poker chips
          and greasy cards
                              --mi pueblo—
                              --mi pueblo—

I wish (Felipe) I lived at the Blue Heaven hotdog shop.

Hoy Brillará una Luz
(A Little Light Will Shine)

hoy brillará una luz
like some madcap gypsy with a crystal ball
una luz sobre nosotros
like some crazy gypsy with a crystal ball
I see three floors up at New Merchant's Hotel
a wino at the window
a wino in a faded green room with bare walls
who sits by the light of one bald bulb
with his chin propped on his fist
and his wobbly elbow on the sill
a wino in his undershirt
this very night in this cold snap
shivering like d.t.'s
it is 20° or below
and this wino sits estúpido at his open window

hoy brillará una luz
after the stores close and I hustle home
Christmas balls and mistletoe
scotch tape curl-tie rickrack

sequins snowflakes foil gift wrap
ticky-tacky bric-a-brac
porque nos ha nacido Señor
just twelve shopping days till Christmas left

tomad y bebed todos de él

tinsel
twinkle stars
jingle bells

porque este es el caliz de mi sangre

telling my fortune to myself

in a room like a cell
in a room like the cops use for third-degree questioning
by the light of one bald bulb
the walls like throw-up
in a room like a rundown hospital
a wino at the window
one dull light and sickroom green
ceilings cracked paint peeling
I stare up and he doesn't see
after my holiday job at MM&G
five and ten or a dollar ninety-nine
and I go on
stiff leg it home
a lonelyhearts show

hoy brillará una luz

my thirsty lips
my frozen hips
selling well are nativity sets
a wino at the window
o Mary
flimsy as angel hair
brittle as ribbon candy
dim as a blue light on a string
o Lady
an upside-down snow scene
held in glass and water bubbling
except for the grace of God I go
dash away dash away dash away all

like some zany gypsy with a crystal ball
I am not sure how to say
or where to keep
what I see.

 ## Salmo 16

Dentro de un Poco
(In a Little While)

Dominican brother peek-a-boo
Martin de Porres brother broom
now in one place now in two
on my dresser your statue
                            Peru Peru
San Martin the stories they tell of you

like a quick-change artist this colored fox
the lone ranger in Texas
Harry Houdini chained in a box
Lima Peru Lima Peru
closed in a monkhouse
but in ports all over the Americas the rich and the riff-raff caught
sight of you
your God-bothered face
                            every place

like Francis of Assisi but in another country
little brother orders rats out of the refectory and shelters them in
an old tool shed

meanwhile bundles abandoned babies and Lima street urchins
into new togs
begs money for medicine and food from the stuffed
founds an orphanage
hither thither
makeshift
this brown-faced Dominican
a man like an apparition
he springs the inside lock somehow from outside and thus
unlatches the door of a viejo's moldy hovel
kneels by a flea-bitten moth-holed pile of blankets
lifts the old one's head up
spoons him a bowl of hot soup while he
el viejo
      disgusting
      consumptive
spews

      --dentro de un poco
      ya no me veréis—

San Martin de Porres peek-a-boo
seven inches tall an Italian statue

this cold night in the rain I am deathly afraid
I squat on the bed with my knees drawn up
I wag my head back and forth like a running-down top
I shiver in a long flannel nightgown like a grandmamma
and jiggle like a half sprung jack-in-the-box

one body

   no body
anybody
   two

this dark night beneath my window
high heels taptapping
as if a boozy late night lady
her spike heels striking the sidewalk   the hatchways
taptapping the ice slicks
and scattering cinders gravel and salt
icicles dripdripping
and twig ends ticking against the window pane
I am deathly afraid to raise my shade
(--se alegró por tanto mi corazón--)
for like a yoyo
like the sudden flame up and the sudden flip down of a butane
lighter
        (--se alegró por tanto--)
it might just be nothing
high heels taptapping
it might just be no one

I am deathly afraid I hear poltergeists
fly-by-night
porque some nights when I sit down in the kitchen
in the dark with only the gas stove lit
when I sit getting warm
I see sneak thieves and cat burglars
(--mi corazón--)
slinking between children's sleepers frozen stiff
on the clothesline

in the corner of my eye
but when I turn full face
          (--y se gozó mi alma--)
no one
nada

San Martin de Porres
one man two
I see ghost shapes San Martin
all over Peru

Lord God I have not the faith of this wonderworker saint
who gives seven hours a day to pray
Lord God I fear that when I lift my shades
when high heels taptap
to look head on for a boozy lady
I will not find   a scrawny rat in the pantry
                  a tired monk who needs a haircut
                  a hungry viejo racked with t.b.
                  o Lord not you
just the crazy clickclack of spike heels over a cellar stepdown hatch
          (--no dejaras mi alma en el Seol--)
the clickclack of spike heels over gravel and ice slick
          (--ni permitiras que tu santa vea corrupción--)
but because I have not the faith of a wonderworker saint I fear I will see

no feet
no legs
no hips waist breasts
no arms or hands
no face

and so
I whisper to you in my sleep.

 ═══════════════════════════════════

Tú Has Probado Mi Corazón
(You Have Probed My Heart)

hotsy totsy Carla
Carla la chistosa
shows off wearing hats like Chiquita Banana
and the drinkers tease us together
--Carla the apple on your hat
why don't you bite it off—
or
--Rosa be Carmen Miranda
wear bunches of grapes pineapple honeydew nectarines strawberries
why not cantaloupe balls in your hair   or passion fruit
or maybe a half gallon of Tropicana orange juice—

because Carla   cackles
                 claps
                 and yackety-yacks
                 stomps and jigs like there were castanets
they tease
--Rosa a basket of fruit on your head—
because I am topsy turvy with Carla the clown

sometimes I hate Carla
but from my mother my father Orlando Luis and María
I have to get away

porque
                            (--tú has probabdo mi corazón
                            me has visitado de noche--)
from my whole crazy family
I must escape
porque

this Carla who is twenty-one drives us to Hellertown
and treats me at Mary's Café to double shots of anything
or sometimes she buys two quarts of beer and steers us up to a
mountaintop
where with the car parked
we chug-a-lug and hum and sass one another and slap
and figure all the secrets of the universe
until something halts me like a stopwatch
(though I have to get away)
something about Carla I do not quite trust
she giggles too much
and one night
        but I think that once I was drunk
something

something like the beat of wings
something like a smothering

I ran out of the car
waving my arms about my head my face

53

as if to keep off claws
as if to sputter up from nearly drowning
I tried to flag down a truck
before Carla caught me up
and rushed us back to the car
shut the hanging door
while I hollered

>--you dope my drink or what
>you witch
>you daughter of a
>escóndeme bajo la sombra de tus alas
>de la vista de los malos que me opréme
>de mis enemigos
>my God
>que buscan mi vida
>Carla what you do to me
>Carla why you point to the sky
>and you are always so nice
>that my skin crawls—

(and my stomach goes upside down
like the wild mouse at Dorney Park
still when I think of it
though I don't know what)

and all she says is you get me fines and hell
a few more times and you get juvey

I wish I would not let Carla
Carla la chistosa
be my bust-out fire escape

but I go like a loco lady
underage to Mary's Café
doing a rumba as if for Xavier Cugat
my feet deadweight in clogs
my head exploding like overripe fruit
in a basket squashed and bruised
my whole body numb
like when you wake up at night and your hand feels like ginger ale
and it won't lift because you
      were asleep on your arm
and that after only a drink or two

sometimes a dacquiri
rum rum rum
and sugary sugary

something about sweet Carla makes me jumpy as a runaway
jittery
queasy
porque
porque
I have to get away

the big dipper the little dipper the mountaintop the truck
the lights on the dashboard
Carla's fingers by the ash glow of her cigarette
and her faraway voice wondering if we should find some guys
or is this all right
all mixed together
and I forget
but sometimes when I see her face or hear her laugh

my stomach does a summersault

sí
todo el mundo
           Rosa dumb
       · my whole head dancing
          sugar plum
chill sweet Carla in her getaway car
(Carla fizzes like Coke in rum)
I fear
something almost
(a loco ghost)
almost
(I cannot guess)
almost that to something I forget
I once said yes.

 **Salmo 18**

Mi Asilo
(My Stronghold)

a rainbow on a winter night

for his small smile
his kindest eyes
a few quick words like all the colors in the sky

the wizard

there is fantasy Dorothy Toto Oz
there is magic over storm and win from loss
forever from Kansas gracias

I am
   past wishingly
      in love

        in love with Juan Tomás

 **Salmo 19**

Mi Roca
(My Rock)

sometimes I feel like the only lioness in a lion's den
like when in the middle of the afternoon I get pinched on the rear end
by a payday drunk at Domenico's newsstand
(Señor mi roca mi alcazar mi libertador)
like around 4 p.m. when Carla and I stopped down to watch
la lanzadera de Belén
the train that shuttles back and forth
from Philadelphia to Bethlehem
sat down on a cement wall
despite the chill
despite the sky was dark
la lanzadera de Belén
three passenger cars to watch

cinders spat from the track
pebbles scattered off the walk
ashes
salt
we sat on a dry spot melted off

then two young studs came prancing up
just out for a Sunday afternoon loll and loaf stopping off at the
hoagie shop
the one with his thick black kinky mane combed high and out
asked
(glad)
--you're all alone—
and clicked
--tsk—

when Carla yawned he came up close behind her back
he put his arms around her neck
he fiddled with her hair
played
his fingers around her throat
she pretended (annoyed)
to choke

the other with mestizo eyes and straight oiled hair
but pygmy nose and pygmy mouth
slithered behind me whispering
--te quiero—
--enamorada—
glided his arms around my shoulders and began to croon
to rock me rock me like a gentle papa
to cradle me like a nursery song
lala la lala la
until almost I was asleep
as he fussed with my hair
and pulled me easy
pulled me back

until he could sit me in his lap
down
I began of all things to drowse
the owl and the pussycat
until almost I was asleep
sitting there cold by the railroad track
the owl and the pussycat went to sea
down
I began to drown
the owl and the pussy cat went to sea in a beautiful pea-green boat
sputtering

and then we ignored them

our two young studs hoofed it off
laughing past rows of garages and warehouse landings
thigh-slapping down by railroad sidings

so Carla and I looked at each other
shrugged
cool as usual Carla had lied
--oh well mi esposo Pablo—
--I mean you know my novio—
and I had said nothing but
--I am too busy—
--I am too tired—

cinders
pebbles
ashes
salt

the white gates lowered across the boulevard
clenched and locked
the crossing bell clanged
and the red lights flashed
toot-toot
choo-choo
chug-chug
we watched the train from Philly
pull around the bend
by Greco's Banana Company and J-J's Sporting Goods
we waited for it to double back again a good half hour
after the last stop station our South Bethlehem

stop
o Lord mi roca
look
snow clouds and cold cement
mi libertador
at our lions our men
listen
woo-woo

by ice as well as fire I may sin
then lackety-lack
o Lord mi roca
o

la lanzadera never came back.

 *Salmo 20*

Si Dios Quiere
(If God Wants)

diciembre
diciembre
at least there are some good things
si Dios quiere

an evening Mass in Spanish and Advent songs
a borrowed hymnbook from Hermana Magdalena
the parochial school kids and the other nuns
afterwards in the church basement a bazaar
and good old clothes at la tienda de ropas usadas

then downtown like a parade
oompahpah oompahpah
los parroquianos go
to candy cane treat at the A&P
banter at the Price-Rite
where a cheap record player blasts Christmas carols en español
--venid fieles todos entonado himnos—
last shopping nights sales at MM&G
hot chocolate at Carraquillo's

a lighting up Santa Claus rosy red-cheeked
and everyone yackety-yacking boricuo fast
and laughing like crazy

by the laundromat like a piñata I come apart
because I see Juan Tomás across the street
in the doorway of Headstart

Juan Tomás of whom I hardly speak
because he seems to me some kind of saint
a cursillisto or a charismatic
and some kind of savior
a mechanic who also runs the parish second-hand clothes shop
gets food for the barrio co-op
registers our hermanos to vote
somehow gets walkers canes and wheelchairs for our old folks
and runs dances for us jovenes at the fire house

wonderful
counselor
Juan Tomás is some kind of miracle worker

si Dios quiere

yesterday
out of nowhere
oompahpah oompahpah
he asked me to some kind of party with the Padre Christmas Eve
and to the pageant put on by Santa Infancia grade eight
later on this week

o God there are some good things

hot chocolate
Juan Tomás

like a piñata I spill apart
oompahpah oompahpah
I feel like a human kaleidoscope
like a pinwheel
a snowflake
like fireworks that go poppoppop in the sky and cascade down
a fountain
like the Moravian decorations uptown
and the star on top of Saucon Mountain
like full organ and orchestra at Packer Chapel
with the whole Lehigh Valley Chorus singing Messiah
      --unto us a child is born
        unto us a son is given—
like a shepherdess before the crib
a seraph singing Gloria

Santa María
si means if
but sí says yes

a sky full of angels

si Dios quiere
this Christmas for me
will be like a sunburst.

Forty-Plus Years Later

Everyone these days seems to call me "Tía." Orlando, Luis, and Maria have made Mama an abuela over and over and me a chuckling, dandling, gift-bearing aunt. And now their kids are having kids.

Mama is a relaxed and fattening widow who does actually walk like a toy, a decelerating top or a weeble-wobble. Papa died years ago, beer in his belly, cigar smoke in his lungs, grease spots all over his work pants, and some comforting regrets in his heart. Mama is all right, as she had secretly saved money, as well as used it for us, for as long as she had worked. Several times a year she goes to the 30ᵗʰ Street Station in Philadelphia and boards a train for Savannah. Believe it or not, I live in a condo outside Hilton Head and am a realtor. The rides to Savannah are for her visits. When Mama comes, we go to the Pinckney Island Wildlife Refuge and watch ibises, blue herons, cormorants, terns, and also the sand crabs scooting along the Intracoastal Waterway. An occasional dolphin rises and smiles.

My two languages and undying wanderlust have helped me to settle big money retirees in flower-studded gated golf communities and also to shelter families spilling over with niños as they wend and wangle their way through immigration and a zillion landscaping and contracting jobs. After Juan Tomás was blown to bits in Viet Nam, I never could quite settle on anyone. I have my Nook, my porch chairs, a pudgy pug, a circle of friends, rum and Coke at night, and a view of the sunrise that stirs me to work or shopping or volunteering or church. It is hard to fathom that I will soon be turning 60 and getting senior rates at Golden Coral and a discount on Wednesdays at Kroger's. Sometimes these things seem enough.

But I still have longings large and faraway as galaxies. And I still find the burger smells and salsas and the grit of the day reason often to smile and sometimes to cry.

Pan y vino, sand and surf and moon-glow breaking from violet blue sky over the needles and cones of tall pines—these things scratch away at things buried in me like jewels in treasure chests and dog bones in mulched backyards. I wonder and hum and sketch and stretch and on Sundays, with Mexicans and Colombians and Ecuadorans, I open *Flor y Canto*, Flower and Song. And so, of course, I sing.

A former boss told me that I am a deeply peaceful person with spitfire spurts. I do not like it when people hurt. Way down, beneath the thrum of tides and cars trembling at stop signs with rap sound, under the smoke that sneaks from behind the off-road rusty trailers of the area's elders who think burning household trash in oil drums after dusk is a necessary rite, I believe an undying heart beats.

And means something.

Escuchanos, Señor.

Somewhere another young woman murmurs and resents and grows fond and lays plans to follow dreams.

Diciembre glitters and is good.

Si Dios quiere.